THE MANUAL

BIBLE NOTES FOR MEN

You 2.0

Getting new Christians started with God, the Bible and faith

CARL BEECH WITH
MARK GREENWOOD

CWR

Carl

Carl Beech is the UK Director of The Message Trust, a charity focused on reaching the hardest-to-reach young people with the message of Jesus. He is also President of CVM (Christian Vision for Men) and has seen it expand into a global movement, working in countries as far afield as Cambodia.

Mark

Mark Greenwood is a northern lad who started out as a butcher. He now travels all around the UK working with men and churches in anything from Indian restaurant evenings to stand-up comedy.

Copyright © Carl Beech 2013

Published 2014 by CWR, Waverley Abbey House, Waverley Lane, Farnham, Surrey GU9 8EP, UK. CWR is a Registered Charity – Number 294387 and a Limited Company registered in England – Registration Number 1990308.

This edition printed in 2017.

The right of Carl Beech and Mark Greenwood to be identified as the authors of this work has been asserted by them in accordance with the Copyright, Designs and Patents Act 1988.

All rights reserved. No part of this publication may be reproduced, stored in a retrieval system, or transmitted, in any form or by any means, electronic, mechanical, photocopying, recording or otherwise, without the prior permission in writing of CWR.

For a list of National Distributors visit www.cwr.org.uk/distributors

All Scripture references are from the Holy Bible: New International Version® Anglicised, NIV® Copyright © 1979, 1984, 2011 by Biblica, Inc.® Used by permission. All rights reserved worldwide.

Concept development, editing, design and production by CWR

Printed in the UK by Linney

ISBN: 978-1-78259-747-6

Contents

A new hope   4

Fruits of the Spirit   14

Telling others   32

Spiritual disciplines   34

A tour of the Lord's Prayer   46
MARK GREENWOOD

More than wise sayings   58

01
You crossed the line

'Flesh gives birth to flesh, but the Spirit gives birth to spirit. You should not be surprised at my saying, "You must be born again."'
John 3:6-7

I vividly remember the moment I gave my life to Jesus Christ. I can also remember the startling range of emotions I felt over the next hour: I cried, I laughed, I jumped up and down and had moments of intense quiet and reflection. What I remember more than anything though is the sensation, standing on the steps of a church in Hornchurch, Essex, of stepping out of a black and white picture into a high definition, full colour picture. It was as if the veil had come off my eyes. Amazing!

In John's Gospel, Jesus is having a chat with a bloke called Nicodemus. He's a Pharisee, which means he was a religious leader and part of a group that didn't like Jesus much at all. As you journey on with Jesus you'll learn a lot about the

Pharisees! Because Jesus was an enemy of the Pharisees, Nicodemus went to see him in secret to find out what was going on. In a nutshell, Jesus tells him that he needs to be born again. I thought that phrase was a bit cheesy when I first heard it. It conjured up images of men wearing socks and sandals, and bad singing in old and mouldy churches. That, however, is far from the case. If you've met Jesus and given your life to Him, you are born again. You have a new start, a new future, new possibilities and a new hope. The adventure has just begun!

Prayer: Thank You Jesus for the new start and new hope that You have given me. Help me to live my life now in a way that honours You. Amen.

02 U-turn

'After John was put in prison, Jesus went into Galilee, proclaiming the good news of God.' **Mark 1:14**

When Jesus first started His public ministry He used to tell people that they needed not just to believe in Him but *repent* as well.

Now that's not a word that you often hear these days. So what does it mean? Basically it means to change direction completely and do a total about turn. In other words, you were living your life with one set of values and now you have turned around and walked away from your old way of life.

A brilliant story to read later is that of Zacchaeus. You can find the story in Luke 19 in the Bible. He was basically a sophisticated thief. Being a chief tax collector he would've done more than just collect the tax money, he was ripping people off as well; to say tax collectors were unpopular would be a massive understatement. One of the most striking things about the story is what he did once he had spent time with Jesus. He didn't just say sorry, he put all the wrongs right. He paid back to people what he had stolen and gave them more as well! That's the sign of a truly changed heart. It's a big challenge that all Christians face: what do we need to repent of and turn away from? And what are we going to do about it?

In other words, repentance is more than feeling sorry for yourself; it's acknowledging that you sinned against God and that you are open to accepting God's forgiveness and help in moving on from that sin. It's one of the most empowering and freeing things we can do because we are demonstrating that we have a new life in Christ.

Prayer: Holy Spirit, change my heart to accept Your forgiveness. Then show me where I have caused offence and give me the strength to put it right. Amen.

03 The first step

'he said to Simon, "Put out into deep water, and let down the nets for a catch." Simon answered, "Master, we've worked hard all night and haven't caught anything. But because you say so, I will let down the nets." When they had done so, they caught such a large number of fish that their nets began to break.'

Luke 5:4-6

Recently I was speaking to some guys about Jesus when a bloke pulled me aside and asked if Jesus could forgive anyone. After I replied that He could, he said, 'So can Jesus forgive a Nazi who gassed Jews to death in a concentration camp?'

'Yes, of course He can!' I replied.

'How does that happen then?'

'When Jesus died on the cross, if the Nazi was genuinely repentant for what he had done,

Jesus took that Nazi's sins on the cross. In other words, He took the hit instead of that guy. Sure there are consequences, but the eternal ones were taken care of.'

The guy got emotional and confessed that he had been part of a far right movement in the UK. The next day he gave his life to Jesus Christ. He was totally struck by the fact that God can truly forgive anyone.

We all have stains and blemishes in our lives. Take time today to thank Jesus for dying for you. Ask Him to show you where you need to change and what you need to put right. It's a lifetime journey but it starts right now! I would also add that the process of 'keeping short accounts' with God is ongoing daily. The closer you get to God over the years the more you will realise just how holy He is compared to you. So many people say things like, 'But I'm a good person; I don't cheat or steal or have affairs.' This may be true but over time we begin to realise just what a dark centre we have. Thank God for Jesus, who makes us clean in front of God!

Prayer: Help me to walk closely before You, God. See if there is anything offensive in me and lead me in the way everlasting (Psalm 139:24). Amen.

04 Messing up

> 'For we do not have a high priest who is unable to empathise with our weaknesses, but we have one who has been tempted in every way, just as we are – yet he did not sin.' **Hebrews 4:15**

Let's cut straight to the point today. One thing is absolutely for sure. You will mess up as a Christian. We're human beings and we aren't perfect. We make mistakes, we lose our cool, we get tempted and we foul up. That's just as inevitable as the fact that you will one day die. The question is more about how we deal with it when we do.

I know so many Christians who beat themselves up for ages when they mess up. They suffer with prolonged guilt and shame and almost go into a spiritual shutdown mode. In a way I guess that's better than just shrugging your shoulders and saying, 'Well it's OK, God forgives me,' but either way doesn't take on board both the cost of Jesus' death and the grace that He shows us.

When we mess up we need to know that we follow Jesus, who was tempted in every way and therefore understands our weaknesses. We kneel before a God who understands us! We can approach with the confidence that He will not condemn us but forgive us... as long as our repentance is genuine. On the other hand, however, we also need to acknowledge the huge cost through which that grace and forgiveness comes. Jesus died so that we can know peace. We shouldn't treat that with disrespect but with honour and deep gratitude. So, in other words, when we mess up we can know God's help and strength. But let's not use that as an excuse not to change.

Prayer: God, help me to remember that You understand me fully and know all my weaknesses. Thank You for the gift of forgiveness and the grace that You show me when I do mess up. Amen.

05
It's not a solo journey

'They devoted themselves to the apostles' teaching and to fellowship, to the breaking of bread and to prayer. Everyone was filled with awe at the many wonders and signs performed by the apostles. All the believers were together and had everything in common. They sold property and possessions to give to anyone who had need. Every day they continued to meet together in the temple courts. They broke bread in their homes and ate together with glad and sincere hearts, praising God and enjoying the favour of all the people.'

Acts 2:42-47

We live in a very individualistic society and we don't really do stuff in 'community' any more. The thing is though; we were built and designed by God to walk through this sensational adventure called life with other people. Genesis, the first book of the Bible, describes how God made man and woman to live together as a unit because 'it's not good for man to be alone' (Genesis 2:18). This is just one of many reasons why there are local churches. The Church is the vehicle that God has put in place, where we learn about Him, grow with other believers in faith and understanding, and reach out to the world. My advice is that you find a church that loves Jesus, follows the teaching found in the Bible, and is working with other churches in its area.

Now, you may not enjoy every meeting it has. But Jesus believes in the Church and therefore so do we because Church is much more than the Sunday meeting. Church is about a community of people who follow Jesus and want others to know about Him. It's at church that you will learn from others, find some new mates and get some encouragement when you feel like chucking in the towel. Life wasn't designed to be a solo journey, so get plugged in and stick with it.

Prayer: Thank You, Jesus, for the local church. Show me how to get involved and help me make some new mates who will help me, as much as I help them, to keep walking with You. Amen.

06

It's all about fruit

'But the fruit of the Spirit is love, joy, peace, forbearance, kindness, goodness, faithfulness, gentleness and self-control. Against such things there is no law.' **Galatians 5:22-23**

There are some key indicators that show whether or not someone is truly walking with Jesus and is filled with the Holy Spirit. They are described as 'the fruit of the Holy Spirit'. In other words, as the power of the Holy Spirit works in your life, you start to see changes in your character that demonstrate that you are being shaped and crafted into someone who acts like Jesus.

The first characteristic of someone who follows Jesus is that he demonstrates love for other people as well as for God. Remember, you now realise that you were worth dying for and that God loves you. Once you know that's true for you, surely you want everyone else to know that? Why? Because they are all God's kids as well. Knowing this starts to have a massive effect on your behaviour. Instead of losing the plot in the car when someone cuts you up or getting into a dispute with a neighbour, you can get past it because you know that Jesus loves them. In the same way that Jesus loves us, we demonstrate that love to others. If we don't do that, the consequence is that we are not really showing love for God. Blunt but true.

Prayer: God, help me to demonstrate that I lead a life characterised by a love for You and for people. Amen.

---

07 Joy is a state of mind

'May the God of hope fill you with all joy and peace as you trust in him, so that you may overflow with hope by the power of the Holy Spirit.' **Romans 15:13**

When you read that we are meant to be people of 'joy' you'll probably be picturing in your mind a kind of weirdo standing there with a cheesy grin on his face who thinks that everything in the world is brilliant, no matter what.

Let me be clear, cheesy-grins and an unrealistic view of the world are not what this is all about. For me it's about having an inner state of mind and heart that knows that eventually everything will work out OK. We know that it will, because as Christians we have access to the last page of the story in the Bible and we know that it's got a happy ending! Of course, rubbish happens.

Of course, life throws up its challenges. Of course, you will have massively grumpy days. That's a part of life, right? The difference for a follower of Jesus is that you can push on past all of that negative stuff because deep in your heart and mind you know that Jesus is for you. You know that one day everything will be alright, even though at the moment you may be passing through a storm. It's that inner joy that helps us keep things in perspective. So don't go to church with a silly grin on your face – you'll just freak people out. But carry with you an inner calm and joy that comes from knowing the Creator of the universe.

Prayer: Lord, create in me an inner calm and an inner joy that comes from knowing that You are for me and that You are walking with me for eternity. Amen.

08 Peacemaker

'Blessed are the peacemakers, for they will be called children of God.'

Matthew 5:9

When I bought my first house in 1994 it was a new build. It was a fantastic pad with one potentially fatal flaw: the builders didn't put fences up. This means that all the new neighbours had to negotiate doing it themselves and work out where the boundaries were. Classic potential for neighbourhood war and there very nearly was one! My neighbours on one side were, shall we say, slightly nit-picking over just where their garden started and finished... to the point where even half an inch became a point of potential stress and conflict. Part of me wanted to dig my heels in because they were being unjust and moaning all the time. It even got to the point where I wanted to avoid them in the mornings and would time getting home to miss them!

Then I hit on a radical solution in a eureka moment. I went round to their house and told them that I would fully fund the fence (even though it was their boundary) and what's more that I would make sure it was more on my side than theirs to make sure I didn't touch their garden. I made this offer whilst offering them a bottle of wine as a gesture of goodwill. The end result was happy neighbours and I lost about an inch of garden. Big deal. One thing was for sure though; losing that inch gave me a lot of peace. And that's the point. We are called to be men of peace. Our testosterone often makes us want to fight. The way of Jesus is to take the countercultural route. Do the opposite to everyone else and watch the world and people change all around you.

Prayer: Help me to take the path of peace and not war when it comes to my friendships, family, work and relationships, God. Amen.

09

Take a deep breath

'take note of this: Everyone should be quick to listen, slow to speak and slow to become angry' **James 1:19**

I'll admit it. Patience is not my strongest point. I'm a fidget. I can't sit still. I want everything to happen now and I tend to move through life at 100 mph. This is both a blessing and a curse for me and for those who are closest to me. Patience is something I constantly have to work on. All I can share is the lessons I have learned so far in my quest to walk humbly before God and sort out the rough edges in my life.

I'm learning that I have a first response to problems and then a second response that's more reasonable and thought through. I therefore bite my tongue more than I used to. I've learnt that actually taking a deep breath is a good thing when I want to snap; it stops me from snapping! Sometimes I just need to calm down and remember that things will happen anyway, even if it's not right now! I try to remember that there are people around me and that life is not just about me and what I need. There is a direct link between impatience and selfishness!

Crucially, there is also a big link between impatience and anger. If you have kids, for example, it's so easy to lose your rag with them but a short vent from us can do more damage than you realise. The same goes for people we work with, as well as other members of our families. That's why God sees this as such an important characteristic. Patience brings life, not hurt and stress.

Prayer: God, give me opportunities this week to be a man of patience. Fashion my character and deal with the rough edges that are at work in this area. Amen.

09

10 Kindness

'Therefore, as God's chosen people, holy and dearly loved, clothe yourselves with compassion, kindness, humility, gentleness and patience.' **Colossians 3:12**

The word 'kind' always sounds a bit bland to me. In fact, if someone is described as a 'kind person' it can almost sound as if that's because they can't think of anything better to say! However, true kindness is far more radical than that. What we need to do is to lead a kindness revolution.

I know a guy who drives a taxi in London. He told me how one day, a guy paid his fare and then handed over an extra £10 with the words: '£5 of this is for you and £5 is for you to pass on to your next fare as a discount or as a freebie... with the condition that they pass on the blessing.' My mate wasn't a Christian but the words and gesture had a profound effect on him. He did as the guy asked and it took the next customer's breath away. An act like that in a selfish world really stands out. Kindness is radical. From speaking a kind word when so much of people's talk is complaint and criticism, to random acts of generosity or dropping everything to help someone, all make the world a very different place indeed. As a man of God you are a leader in the kindness movement. So go to it and enjoy it. The thing is that the kinder you are, the more it affects your own heart; it changes you too!

Prayer: Lord, show me times this week when I can practise the art of radical kindness. Mould me and shape me so that it becomes instinctive to me. Amen.

11

Goody two-shoes

'Surely your goodness and love will follow me all the days of my life, and I will dwell in the house of the LORD forever.' **Psalm 23:6**

What is 'goodness'? It kind of conjures up images of the goody two-shoes kid at school that used to grass you up when you were messing around. Or the guy in the office who's always creeping around the boss and manipulating the system to get the promotion. Either that, or it just sounds really, really twee.

Obviously though, it's meant to be far deeper and impacting than that. Goodness is about the way you view the world and handle your interactions with people. Let's nail this by asking some questions: do you give the benefit of the doubt or always have a cynical take on things? Do you believe the best in all circumstances, or the worst? Do you go the extra mile for people, or take short cuts wherever you can? Do you hang in there with those who are struggling, or give up?

You see, goodness is a state of being that flows through the whole of your life. It's driven by selflessness and the overwhelming knowledge that you have been saved by the grace of God; something you didn't earn or deserve. In other words, God has been so good to us that we live a life of goodness and gratitude ourselves. We can practise being good and do good things, but at the end of the day, it truly is a state of being.

Prayer: Thank You, God, that You are good. Create in me a good and grace-filled heart towards all those I interact with. Amen.

12 You gotta have faith

'Let love and faithfulness never leave you; bind them around your neck, write them on the tablet of your heart. Then you will win favour and a good name in the sight of God and man.' **Proverbs 3:3-4**

Faithfulness is a priceless commodity in a 'grab it, get it, do what you need to do' world. It's not just about being faithful in a marriage or relationship (although that is hugely important) but in every area of your life. The thing is though, that being faithful isn't as easy as it sounds. If it was easy, people wouldn't shipwreck marriages by going off with someone else and friends would never stab each other in the back. Business deals would always be honoured after a shake of hands and no one would lie to anyone.

So what makes it so tough? It's the old fashioned word 'sin' that's at the heart of it. Sin is self-centredness. It's when everything becomes about you and not Jesus or other people. That really is the secret. Live for God and for other people and the funny thing is that life becomes richer and more fulfilling. Live for yourself and things generally start to unravel. Put it to the test. How many tight fisted people have loads of friends? How many cheaters do you trust? As with most kingdom of God living, it really does boil down to basic principles that lead to a full-on and joy filled life. Keep the faith and stay faithful.

Prayer: God, please guard my heart and strengthen me to stay faithful in all my actions and words. Amen.

---

13 Gently does it

'Take my yoke upon you and learn from me, for I am gentle and humble in heart, and you will find rest for your souls.' **Matthew 11:29**

Clearly I'm stating the totally obvious here when I tell you that I'm a bloke. On the surface at least, I'm probably a cliché man. I'm a petrol head and I love cars, bikes, planes and, in fact, anything with an engine. I like to lift weights, run marathons, watch rugby and have huge bonfires. There is, however, another side to me: I have two daughters and watch chick flicks with them. I have spent years as a pastor of a church and spent many quiet moments with people who are grieving or suffering with serious illness. In other words, despite my testosterone levels, I can be tender and gentle, too.

Being gentle doesn't mean you have to act like a complete sap. It's a sign of a different sort of strength and one that is much needed. The opposite of gentleness would be uncontrolled aggression and rage. I say uncontrolled, because I do think that there is a place for a righteous anger. More on this later in the book. For now, however, just take note that those who have been impacted by the love and grace of God should demonstrate an ability to be gentle and tender. As you read through the Gospels you will notice there were times when Jesus could be hugely confrontational. But there were also times when He stopped to talk with children, spent time with those who were broken, healed the sick, and wept over the condition of people. To be able to do these things is to be a real man.

Prayer: Jesus, create a gentle side to my nature. Build within me a strength that is also demonstrated in tenderness and gentleness towards people. Amen.

---

14 Self-control

'For the Spirit God gave us does not make us timid, but gives us power, love and self-discipline.' **2 Timothy 1:7**

Every year I chuck into my schedule something that will require me to exercise a lot of self-discipline. Usually this involves doing stuff that I don't instinctively like (otherwise I wouldn't need lots of self-discipline to do it!) I set a target, make it public, and therefore get held to it. So what sort of things have I done? I've cycled from Land's End to John O'Groats in nine days, as well as Calais to Nice over the Alps, and pretty much the length of Italy. I've run a marathon and am currently days away from running the toughest marathon in Europe, which involves lots of running across a mountain range! Why? Not because I'm a fitness junky, but because I need to practise discipline or I could all too easily get lazy, lardy and out of shape physically, as well as spiritually and emotionally.

When you have to go on training runs up hills in the cold and rain, it starts to do something to you. It changes your mindset.

You find a new ability to rein in all sorts of temptations and desires. It's good to have periods where you get a grip on stuff. I don't have a problem with alcohol but that's because I know that I could, and so have periods where I don't touch a drop at all. I want to know that I am master over things that could control me. What about you? What disciplines have you put into your life or think that you should put in place?

Prayer: Father, give me discipline in the areas of my life where I need more self-control. Amen.

14

15 Go!

'Therefore go and make disciples of all nations, baptising them in the name of the Father and of the Son and of the Holy Spirit, and teaching them to obey everything I have commanded you. And surely I am with you always, to the very end of the age.' **Matthew 28:19-20**

As a man who has met Jesus, you have discovered the story of the universe. You know now that this life isn't it, and that there is a life to come that is bigger and more dynamic than this one. You know that you can live life to all its fullness now with Jesus' help. You also know that you are not alone but have a Father in heaven who loves you. All of that is just the tip of the iceberg. Pretty good, isn't it!

But you also now know that for those who don't know Jesus there is potentially bad news. The only way to God is through Jesus, which means that there is an urgent task in front of us to make Jesus known to those around us. This is what we call evangelism. We can make Jesus known to people in all kinds of ways; by behaving differently to others, by showing compassion and kindness, by being more generous than others and caring for those who are struggling or finding life tough. All of this is good. However, there is still a need to actually tell people or they'll just think that you are a very nice bloke!

One of the best bits of advice I have been given since I gave my life to Jesus was to tell people about Him and what has happened to me. This does two very cool things. Firstly, it gives people a chance to hear the good news about Jesus from someone whose life has been radically transformed. Secondly, it helps you to make your faith feel more real to yourself. The bottom line is this: Jesus has told us to share our faith and to make Him known to others. So let's pray for opportunities and go for it. Remember, though, that you were once on a journey to faith, and it may have taken a long time to get there! Show the same patience to others, but don't hold back when the opportunity arises!

Prayer: Please God, create for me an opportunity to share my faith today and give me the courage to do so when that moment happens. Amen.

16

Prayer

'And pray in the Spirit on all occasions with all kinds of prayers and requests. With this in mind, be alert and always keep on praying for all the Lord's people.' **Ephesians 6:18**

One of the biggest and most amazing privileges we have is the ability to talk to God whenever we want to. Think about it. We have the opportunity to dialogue with the Creator of the universe. Pretty mind blowing really. Not only that, but you soon start to realise that He really does answer prayer. Granted, not always in the way we expect Him to, but He does answer! So how should we go about praying on a regular and daily basis?

As I have to travel a lot for work it's hard for me to have routines, so I've developed a habit of prayer that works for me. You will need to do the same for yourself. I'm a fidget, so I tend to pray on the move as well as during random moments in the day. I make sure, though, that I pray quietly at some point every day. I take time in those moments to both speak and listen. I used to find that my mind wandered. An easy solution for this is to pray out loud. Bible notes also help you to focus on God at the start of the day. Of course, I want to recommend the follow-up series to this book: *The Manual*!

So what do I do? Well, when I'm at home I walk my dog every morning and I pray for certain people and situations. There are some people that I pray for every single day. I also thank God a lot for things in my life that are a true blessing. I think God really likes it when we say thank You and remember times when He has helped us. I also pray when I'm in the car on the way to meetings, during meetings, and pretty much whenever... it's a lifestyle, not a single moment at a fixed time. Another thing that's helped me is reading the Psalms in the Bible. These are prayers and worship songs to God and they are pretty amazing. Reading those really will help develop depth to your prayer life. Prayer is about you building a relationship with God. Over time, I guarantee that you'll grow to love it.

Prayer: Lord, help me to build times of prayer into my life. Help me to learn how to hear Your voice. Meet with me during the times of quiet I spend with You and during the busy times as well. Amen.

---

17 Fasting

'When you fast, do not look sombre as the hypocrites do, for they disfigure their faces to show others they are fasting. Truly I tell you, they have received their reward in full. But when you fast, put oil on your head and wash your face, so that it will not be obvious to others that you are fasting, but only to your Father, who is unseen; and your Father, who sees what is done in secret, will reward you.'

Matthew 6:16-18

So what's all this about? You become a follower of Jesus and suddenly you're told not to eat?! It's another kind of spiritual discipline and one that Jesus expects us to do. In the Bible verse, notice that he says 'when you fast', not 'if you fast'.

So why do it? Well, firstly it directs your focus to God. Every time you feel like eating is a reminder to pray. Secondly, it helps us to remember how fragile and dependent on God we really are. Thirdly, fasting has spiritual power. In the Bible, there are times when people fasted and huge spiritual battles were fought in 'the heavenly places'. For an example of this, see Daniel chapter 10 in the Old Testament.

It's kind of up to you how you go about it. Perhaps once or twice a month you could miss lunch at work and go for a prayer walk. Maybe you could build up to taking a whole day to fast (as long as there are no medical reasons why this wouldn't be a good idea). Maybe you could abstain for a period of time from alcohol and rich foods, and just keep a simple diet. These periods of time can be amazing and really help you to get closer to God. Ironically, it's the hungry for God who tend to fast the most! One final word of advice though – just remember it's not a hunger strike.

Prayer: God, put some steel and grit in my spirit and help me to buckle down to some serious times of prayer and fasting. Amen.

18

Give up some dosh

'Now about the collection for the Lord's people: Do what I told the Galatian churches to do. On the first day of every week, each one of you should set aside a sum of money in keeping with your income, saving it up, so that when I come no collections will have to be made.'
1 Corinthians 16:1-2

In the Old Testament, God's people knew that they were truly dependent on God for everything. As a way of acknowledging this, they would set aside, at various times of the year, the best of their crops or livestock and give it back to God. They called it a tithe. Typically it amounted to 10% of what they had.

In the New Testament, we're told to set aside a sum of money in keeping with our income and give it to God's work. I know what you're immediately asking: how much should this be? Well, perhaps you could use 10% as a kind of guideline. If you're not used to giving then perhaps you could build up to it over a period of time. What I do know is that it's not really optional.

I think it's also important that we don't ignore the developing world and those who are suffering in poverty. My wife and I sponsor a couple of children in India and Africa as part of our response to that need. We also give to our church and to an organisation that works in evangelism. We've adjusted our lifestyle so that we can give because we feel that being part of God's family needs to be more than just words. We should put our money where our mouth is. The thing is, there is a huge amount of need out there and the resources are available; they're just in the wrong places! As a footnote, I'm fully aware that some people reading this won't have much money or will be out of work. What I am sharing here is a principle to work towards.

Prayer: Father, create in me a generous and giving heart. Show me where to give my money towards Your work. Amen.

19
Justice

'The Spirit of the Lord is on me,
because he has anointed me
to proclaim good news to the poor.
He has sent me to proclaim
freedom for the prisoners
and recovery of sight for the blind,
to set the oppressed free' **Luke 4:18**

These verses have had a profound impact on
my life over the years. Right at the start of Jesus'
public ministry He states what the heart of His
mission is; to heal the sick, set people who are
spiritually captive free, spread the good news of
the kingdom, and show mercy and God's love
to the poor. Take the theme of justice out of the
Bible and you have a very thin Bible indeed. The
thing is this, we are called to follow Jesus in this
and have a heart for justice as well. So how do we
do this, beyond giving our money?

It could be that we reappraise how we spend
our time. Could you use your skills to make a
positive impact in your community? Are there

projects you could get involved in, or even start? One group of men that I met recently give a few hours a month to help people who are elderly or suffering long term ill-health decorate their houses. Another group I know get alongside guys who have just come out of prison. Some people have used their skills on a short term trip overseas to a help renovate an orphanage. The options are endless. The important thing is that we do something. It's all part of being a man of God.

Prayer: Jesus, please show me how I can get involved in my community or elsewhere to make a difference. Give me a heart for justice and caring for those with far less than me. Amen.

20

Armour up!

'Finally, be strong in the Lord and in his mighty power. Put on the full armour of God, so that you can take your stand against the devil's schemes.' **Ephesians 6:10-11**

When you gave your life to Jesus, several amazing things happened simultaneously. Your destiny was secured, you were forgiven, you received the Holy Spirit, and you were given the chance to lead a whole new life. Amazing! Some other things happened as well though. You immediately got a bull's-eye on your back and you became an open declaration of war against the forces of darkness.

As followers of Jesus Christ we also believe in a personal force of evil we call the devil. We believe that he is set against us and that he hates God with a brutal anger that is hard to fully comprehend. We know that he wants to hurt God and he will do so by attacking those whom God loves. Such as you!

The Bible often speaks of the battle that we're engaged with and it tells us repeatedly how to take our stand against evil. In this passage we are told that we should put on the full armour of God so that we can stand against the enemy. Our defensive weapons are truth, righteousness, the peace of the gospel, faith, and knowing we are saved. Then there's one offensive weapon: the Bible is described as the sword of the Spirit (Ephesians 6:17, explored tomorrow). That's why it's so important to have a time when you read the Bible every day. Make that time – try not to skip it. That's why the character stuff we've looked at such as 'the fruit of the Spirit' is so important... because those things shield us. We're in a battle. Let's fight it well.

Prayer: I take my stand against the enemy and his schemes and strategies. I ask You, Father, to fill me with Your Holy Spirit and constantly shield me with Your armour. Amen.

---

21 Using the sword

'Take the helmet of salvation and the sword of the Spirit, which is the word of God.' **Ephesians 6:17**

So how should we read the Bible? Personally, I keep a Bible app on my phone because I find it useful to be able to call up a verse or have a quick look every so often during the day. It's also useful when you get into a chat with someone about Jesus.

I also think it's good to try and set some time aside each day for a bit of a longer read (not necessarily for hours because even five or ten minutes can be good) followed by a prayer. A great tip, as well as using notes like this, is to get hold of a Bible reading plan that takes you through the whole Bible in a year (there are two great ones available from www.cwr.org.uk/bible).

The bottom line is that the Bible is spiritual food. I can tell who is reading it regularly because they just behave differently. The Bible is becoming part of them. It's more than a book. It's God's living Word to us today and every day. My advice is to get into the habit now and set yourself up for the long term.

I remember one time when I was under such huge pressure, that all I read was Psalm 139. I read it so much that now I can recall it at will and recite it whenever I want. In other words, there's no law about how and when you read it. Just make sure that you do.

Prayer: God, give me a passion and desire to read Your Word and help me to absorb the truths in the Bible into my character and heart. Amen.

22

My dad's bigger than your dad

'Our Father in heaven'

'The Spirit you received does not make you slaves, so that you live in fear again; rather, the Spirit you received brought about your adoption to sonship. And by him we cry, "Abba, Father."' **Romans 8:15**

You're seven years old and you've hit the classic line that probably every lad has said in the school playground, 'Well, my dad's bigger than your dad'. I used to say it hoping that this claim would never be put to the test! Sadly my kids can't say this with real conviction - I'm only 5 foot 5! Mind you, it's the little ones you've got to watch!

One of things you will learn more the longer you stick with God is that our Dad really is the most powerful and strongest of all. Remember,

whatever you face, God is bigger. It gets better –
He's awesome but He's personal.

One of the great sadnesses I see as I travel this
country is dads who are brilliant people and who
are admired by their kids. They do lots for them,
but they aren't personal with them. This isn't true
of God – He's both amazing and personal.

Let's celebrate that He's our Father – that's family.
The challenge is to make sure we don't become
so blasé about the personal aspect that we
lose sight of the fact that He's powerful. Then
again, we don't want to just see God as a God
Who can do things and not enjoy our Father-son
relationship with Him. We miss out on all that God
has if we just come to Him when we need Him for
something.

**Prayer: Father God, help
me to get the balance right
in how I see You. Help me
to totally respect You but
personally know You. Amen.**

23

Walkie-talkie lifestyle

'hallowed be your name'

'Whoever claims to live in him must live as Jesus did.' **1 John 2:6**

I've a friend – not just one! – and whenever I think of this friend a smile comes to my face. I also know people that make me feel sad or angry when I think of their names. There are certain feelings and reactions we have when a name is mentioned.

Whenever I think of God's name the reaction should be honour. The word 'hallowed' means treated with the highest honour. Linked with yesterday's reading, Jesus is expressing concern that our heavenly Father's name is treated with the highest honour and respect.

I feel pressure when I'm recommended by fellow evangelists to speak somewhere as it's their name and reputation that's also at stake. I want to protect their name. We protect, and therefore honour,

God's name in the way we live just as much as we do in any kind of sung worship or spoken prayer.

It's worth remembering that old adage – let our walk match our talk. I want it to be as obvious that I honour and respect God when I'm out with my mates who don't know God as when I'm in with my mates who do. There should be a consistency in our words and actions.

As I claim to worship His name in words I should also do so in actions. As you grow in your Christian journey be aware of the ways in which you honour or don't honour God's name. How can you and I treat God's name with the highest honour?

Prayer: God, I want You to know that I respect Your name. Help me to show this in the way I live. Amen.

---

24 Better out than in!

'your kingdom come'

'For the kingdom of God is not a matter of eating and drinking, but of righteousness, peace and joy in the Holy Spirit.' **Romans 14:17**

Before I had kids and when my wife worked, we had money. We spent a lot of money (too much) on takeaways. The call always ended with the promise of the order being delivered in 'about thirty minutes'. So after an hour had passed and there was no trace of said food, and after the disappointment of many a car headlight, I'd ring up. The answer was always the same: 'Just coming now, sir.' Sometimes I thought it would be best to just go and get it.

There's a danger whenever we talk about God's kingdom that it's something that's on its way – something that will come to us. It's worth noting that after 'your kingdom come' is 'your will be done'. The day I said yes to God, He came and lived in me – that means that I was part of the kingdom of heaven – but I believe we bring about God's kingdom when we do His will.

The presence of God's kingdom in this age refers to the reign of Christ in the hearts and lives of believers, and to the reigning presence of Christ in His body, the Church – so that they increasingly reflect His love, obey His laws, honour Him, do good for all people, and proclaim the good news of the kingdom.

It's not just something external waiting to break in; it's something internal waiting to break out.

Prayer: Lord, help me to realise that Your kingdom is in me and that I need to let it out by living to Your kingdom principles. Amen.

24

25

Carb up – you'll need the fuel

'Give us today our daily bread'

'I can do all this through Him who gives me strength.' **Philippians 4:13**

I like eating! My favourite meal is curry and my favourite curry is buffet! I've learned the art of using cucumber as scaffolding for getting more into my salad bowl at Pizza Hut. I don't know why I feel I have to do it as I can go back again at any point. That said, it's immensely satisfying seeing people watch me as I navigate my way back to my seat! I've decided that food is great!

When I did my first long hill ride my friend Haydn said to me, 'Carb up, you'll need the fuel.' This was music to my ears. However, the elation of the extra quiche faded after he put me through my paces – I visited some very emotional places that day, but I had just about enough fuel for the ride.

I love the thought behind the words 'Give us today our daily bread'. As bread was the staple diet of the day the sentiment is, 'God, could you give me what I need to get me through today?' This verse righty applies to all our physical needs but actually applies to the whole of our life.

I want to encourage you in your new found faith to develop a good ethic of serving God – but carb up! Make sure the more you do for God the more you ask of God and feed on God.

Let me also encourage you to do more with what you have already received. By the way, I'm not talking about running yourself into the ground, I'm talking about healthy balance.

Prayer: God, please meet my physical needs and my spiritual needs today. May You be my strength in all I do. Amen.

26

I know what you used to be like!

'forgive us our sins'

'If we confess our sins, he is faithful and just and will forgive us our sins and purify us from all unrighteousness.' **1 John 1:9**

So you've become a Christian and you're telling your mates and family about what God's done for you. You're doing well and then they hit you with, 'Yeah, but I know what you used to be like!'

Many people tell me they find the hardest place to share their faith is with mates and family. Don't be freaked – the very fact that they know what you used to be like shows they've seen the change.

My dad became a Christian and at the time didn't feel any different. The following day at work one of his colleagues asked, 'Jim, you okay?'

'Yeah, why?' said Dad.

'Well you've been at work for a few hours and you haven't sworn!'

When you are reminded of what you did, remind yourself it's what you *did*. When you said 'Yes' to God He forgave you what you did! Asking God daily to forgive you is something different. Before you became a Christian you were separated from God – asking God for forgiveness at that point allowed God to take away the separation.

Asking God to forgive you now is a gratitude thing and a 'sorry' thing. You're so grateful for your new found relationship with God that you don't want anything to mess it up.

I love my wife and if I do anything to wrong her I don't want it to get between us, so I make sure I say sorry (okay, confession time – not always as quickly as I should!).

Prayer: God, thank You that I'm forgiven. Help my love for You to increase so that I won't want anything to get in the way. Amen.

27

Forgiveness: what's in it for me?

'as we forgive those who sin against us'

'Then Peter came to Jesus and asked, "Lord, how many times shall I forgive my brother or sister who sins against me? Up to seven times?" Jesus answered, "I tell you, not seven times, but seventy-seven times."' `Matthew 18:21-22`

I'm told I can be a bit defensive, to which I say, 'No I'm not!' and that just makes me look like I am! The truth is I'm not – I just don't like being misunderstood and misrepresented.

I find forgiveness both easy and hard, depending upon how much it affects me emotionally. Being misrepresented or misunderstood affects me deeply, so that's harder. There are some people I regularly have to work at forgiving – man it can be hard! Some of their words ring around my head to this day.

I wrote a talk called 'Forgiveness: what's in it for me?' My research showed links have been made between hostility and heart disease. People who've been able to forgive see their blood pressure go down, their resting heart rate decrease and their immune system get stronger. Forgiveness can alleviate IBS, headaches, backaches, neck pain and strengthen sexual drive.

What forgiveness have you received and what forgiveness do you need to offer? If we fully appreciate what God has forgiven us for, I think we will find forgiveness a bit easier.

By the way, the principle here isn't maths – it is to keep on forgiving! My own experience is that this is easier to say than it is to do, but let's keep the determination to forgive.

Prayer: Lord, help me to become more thankful for what You have forgiven me for, so that it becomes easier to forgive those I need to forgive. Amen.

28

The counter-cultural attitude

'You have heard that it was said, "Love your neighbour and hate your enemy." But I tell you, love your enemies and pray for those who persecute you, that you may be children of your Father in heaven. He causes his sun to rise on the evil and the good, and sends rain on the righteous and the unrighteous. If you love those who love you, what reward will you get? Are not even the tax collectors doing that? And if you greet only your own people, what are you doing more than others? Do not even pagans do that?' **Matthew 5:43-48**

Some of the most important teaching in the whole Bible is found in what we call the Beatitudes in Matthew 5. Here're a few snippets to help you start thinking in a massively counter-cultural way. Make no mistake, this teaching is gritty and tough and when followed properly, cuts to the heart.

What do you do when someone makes an unjust or false accusation against you? I'm sure we've all been on the receiving end of this kind of stuff and it makes your blood boil. If you're anything like me, every cell in your body and every bit of testosterone starts to burn for revenge or to have your say.

Well, Jesus says something here that just cuts to the very heart of the matter. He tells us to love our enemies! More than that, He even tells us to pray for them. Now get this, He isn't telling us to pray that they get eaten by a pack of wolves or spontaneously combust. Jesus is telling us to pray for their absolute best and to be blessed. Stick in your throat? Welcome to the counter cultural world of living life as a man of God. It takes some guts. See also Matthew 5:11-12 for some more hard hitting truth.

Prayer: Help me to take the higher path of living life as a kingdom man, Lord. Even when everything in me is screaming for revenge, give me the peace that comes from doing it Your way and not my way. Amen.

29

Sex drive

'You have heard that it was said,
"You shall not commit adultery." But
I tell you that anyone who looks
at a woman lustfully has already
committed adultery with her in his
heart.' Matthew 5:27-30

Ok, let's start by being a bit real here. If you have
a penis and a pulse you're quite likely to feel the
forces of lust in your life at some point. Some
more than others of course, but the pressure and
power of sexual temptation are real for everyone.

The Old Testament teaching on adultery was
pretty clear. It was a case of 'don't engage in
the physical act'. Jesus, as ever, takes it a notch
further and then some. He goes right to the heart
issue of the problem and identifies adultery as
something that begins in the heart and mind
of a man. As far as Jesus sees it, as soon as you
look at a woman with less than pure intention,
adultery has happened. Ouch! If this is an area of
weakness for you then take action to make sure

that what's going on in your head doesn't take you to places that you don't want to go.

These days, avenues for going astray in these areas are far too accessible. Thirty seconds on the internet and you can have free and pretty full-on hard-core pornography in front of your eyes. There are even dating sites to help you commit adultery. Opportunities are everywhere.

So what do I do to stay on the straight and narrow? Well, I pray that God will keep me strong. I also have an accountability group, which is a group of guys that meet regularly. We laugh together (a lot), we eat food and get radically honest with each other and we open up our lives to scrutiny. There's software you can use to monitor your computer as well (check out covenanteyes.com). All of these things are great tools to help you stay on track. Fight hard and stay on the narrow path of Matthew 7. There's so much to lose if we don't.

Prayer: Help me, God, to be a man with a pure heart and clean hands. Place good men around me who I can journey with. Lead me not into temptation but deliver me from evil. Amen.

---

30 Needy bloke!

'Blessed are the poor in spirit,
for theirs is the kingdom of heaven.'
Matthew 5:3

Us blokes tend to think of ourselves as all sufficient, all capable and in no need of a crutch in life. That's a big mistake.

When you gave your life to Jesus it was a radical commitment to *surrender* your life to Jesus and acknowledge that you need Him. I sometimes wonder just how much we appreciate what Jesus has done for us. Jonathan Edwards, a great preacher of old, painted a picture of people who deserved hell, but hung by a mere thread of God's grace in safety. Without Jesus we were destined for destruction. Without the work of the Holy Spirit in our lives, we can't truly know what life to the full is.

Getting practical about it, every day when I'm at home I walk my dog. When I go on these walks I make it a point to pray. As part of this time of prayer, I thank God for another day of life. I thank

Him for my family and my friends. I thank Him that I have clothes on my back and food to eat. Why? Because knowing your need of God starts by acknowledging that it's in the small things as well as the big things that you need Him.

When I landed my first job in a bank, I really gave myself a massive pat on the back for landing a top job as a young graduate. That Sunday, a man called Morris in my church came over and whispered in my ear, 'Don't forget to thank God... He is the one who gave you the job.' I was pretty miffed at that. After all, it was me, wasn't it? I did it. I smashed the interview and dazzled everyone. I got the degree and worked hard. It was only as I grew in my faith I realised just how right Morris was. Without God, I have very little to offer.

Remember that and you won't go far wrong. The poor in spirit are those who know their need of God. The kingdom of heaven belongs to those guys.

Prayer: Lord, keep me humble and keep my ego in check. Help me to acknowledge my dependency on You. May people see in me a man of the kingdom and not a man who is full of his own self-importance. Amen.

Continue building your relationship with God

Lay the foundations of Christianity and build your relationship with God. Packed with 30 relevant Bible readings, practical points and prayers, these notes will help you navigate through your life and faith.

These Bible notes explore different themes to encourage and challenge. Written by Carl Beech and two guest contributors, each book contains two months of daily readings and prayers.

 Also available in eBook formats

For current prices and to discover the full range, visit
www.cwr.org.uk/themanual